VIRAL

VIRAL

Suzanne Parker

Alice James Books
Farmington, Maine

10 9 8 7 6 5 4 3 2 1

Alice James Books are published by Alice James Poetry Cooperative, Inc.,
an affiliate of the University of Maine at Farmington.

Alice James Books
238 Main Street
Farmington, ME 04938
www.alicejamesbooks.org

Library of Congress Cataloging-in-Publication Data
Parker, Suzanne, 1968-
    [Poems. Selections]
    Viral / Suzanne Parker.
       pages   cm
    Poems.
    ISBN 978-1-938584-01-5 (Pbk.: alk. paper)
    I. Title.
    PS3616.A747V57 2013
    811'.6—dc23   2013014948

Alice James Books gratefully acknowledges support from individual donors,
private foundations, the University of Maine at Farmington, and
the National Endowment for the Arts.

ART WORKS.
arts.gov

Cover illustration by Mary Austin Speaker.

CONTENTS

III

ACKNOWLEDGMENTS

I am grateful to the editors of the following journals in which versions of these poems appeared:

7 Carmine: "Little Boy and Mother"
Bloom: "The Sparrow Lifts the Spent Condom into the Air" and "Practice I"
Drunken Boat: "Passage" and "Splash"
Hunger Mountain: "Viral," "Just," "Phone Call," "Waiting (Day 3)," "Stopped I," "Tunnel," "Gawker.com," and "Bringing Him Back"
The Sierra Nevada Review: "The Physics of Safety"

Over the years, many teachers and friends have generously supported me. To all of them, thank you. In particular, I owe much to Ken Hart, Michael Broek, Mihaela Moscaliuc, Chad Sweeney, Jennifer Kaminski, Nancy Gannon, the Urban Park Rangers, and the late William Matthews who have all shaped my writing in important ways, and, of course, to David and my family. Much gratitude to the Cooperative Board of Alice James Books, to Carey Salerno and Meg Willing for shepherding this book into existence, and to Laura McCullough for her editorial advice, insights, and endless encouragement. Thanks as well to my Grind compatriots who first read many of these poems and kept me writing and to Ross White for bringing us all together. And, always, for everything, Lori.

For Tyler Clementi

That I was, I knew was of my body—and what I should be,
I knew I should be of my body.
　　　—Walt Whitman,
　　　　　"Crossing Brooklyn Ferry"

Anyone with iChat, I dare you to video chat me between the
hours of 9:30 and 12. Yes it's happening again.
　　　—Dharun Ravi,
　　　　　former Rutgers University student,
　　　　　September 21, 2010

Im sorry who the fuck is Tyler Clementi? Yes I do know who
he is he's that pussy fag who hopped off a bridge why is his
roomate on trial?
　　　—Comrade Crank,
　　　　　comment posted following a story on
　　　　　The Huffington Post

If the Body Could Live without Desire

I would be as song
flowing past
hands as in air.
I'd kiss you softly on the ear's rim
and disappear.

Peeping Tom

*After the first time, an invitation was sent to watch again
via webcam.*

One is perversion, pornography,
suspiciously close to whacking off.
There is a history for this.
A man, nearly always, shrugging
across the ground toward a car's steamed window
or the neighbor, hard against the garden hose,
catching snatches of ass and thigh.

Two is a confederacy,
illicit as a knife sliding down the fold
of someone else's letter.
An enactment like Simon Says:
Place tongue here. Place hope there.

Three is the trifecta:
One to laugh. Another to grab the snacks.
A final third to feel a little guilty.

Four. Four's a party. Invitations were sent.
Chairs pulled up. Someone messes
with a playlist. Each time hair is touched—
drink! Complaints arise:
warm beer, poor picture quality, the G-rated
fumblings—two men on a bed,
one still with glasses on.

The boy on the left is thinking: *Fuck.*
We share a fuckin shower.
The girl on the right: *I always wondered.*
The one in the middle,
who opened the secret eye,
is already hoping to take it
live another night.

The Color Blue

The beach is simply the breath held
before diving. He can hold it longer
than needed and does, hold it,
until the darkness cracks.

Lungs swollen with cement,
throat choked, he counts eight years
in heartbeats then explodes
into the future, gasping and rolling
so the sun may dry his face.

The beach is just a rest stop.
Mothers are band-aids, cold drinks in coolers.
The boy loves a certain late afternoon hour
the way, later, beneath his lover
he will cry out as his body splits

and gulls rise from his opened mouth.
Their strong wings stroke the deep
blue distance and call,
testing his desire to return.

Practice I

"It is something else," the man says,
"when your own son chooses violin
over football." Nothing another's
sons would do: their desire
to lean themselves onto huddled
shoulders, the thick of slingshot bodies,
to crash, collapse—flesh, helmet, bone
hammered to the ground.
They lift themselves into the embracing air,
shake off the world, fasten on the next play.

No, you are supportive, of course,
see the rumor around his eyes.
Something suspicious
in all that fingering, head tucked
into the shoulder as if expecting a blow,
that shudders the air in the belly
of the instrument. "There is
something else," you say, "that makes music."

One late summer day,
a rare game in the backyard
spent silent but for advice and retort.
Your thick hand cradles the ball.
Your son is on the ground where you

have put him but reach out
and feel a hardness—
calluses capping every finger—

and you hear that phrase, three notes,
how they lift and lift and lift
yet never take flight, not for hours,
months locked behind the door,
pressed into the skin.

You toss the football in the garage,
call his brothers—
who spend their days between pester
and bellowing—out to the car,
back it out the drive. You pull away
so your son will have some time to practice.

Little Boy and Mother

His mother's head is turned,
busy with sandwiches.
He looks once
around the pool,
checking traffic,
then he's off:
squeals at the rough cement
that slaps his feet,
slaloms the wet tiles,
is halfway to the deep end
with its delicious blue water.
Children stuck
to their chairs gasp
at this jailhouse break,
this defensive threading
through their mothers' hands.
He's got one moment more,
at best. The lifeguard
has already lifted
the whistle from his chest.
His mother spins
on her chaise,
warning swells her lips
as she sees her son vault—
one atom ahead of his name.

Practice II

"I'm practically asexual," posted Tyler Clementi on a gay meet-up site.

Do you think it's easy,
practicing not
to touch?
Subways, check-out lines,
even the passing
of change—
a thumb's extravagant cushion,
fingernails like birds' feet
skittering across the skin.
Try refusing it.
How the eyes must sink,
hold only the ground.

Splash

The body has longed for this:
to dress in slightly more fitted clothes,
take the keys, drive for many miles,
pay for gas, tolls, parking, and the $8 beer
held like an anchor against the tides.
On a bar top, a man, stripped to underwear,
varnished with sweat, moves his hips
as if pressing them into tomorrow,
wraps an arm like a caress
around his face—here,
where there are only men.
It's the thick callous
on the man's palm against
the back of the body's neck,
a place hidden as a fort
built in high, swaying branches.
They are in a bar and a man is wet
from the bucket raining down,
a hundred shatters of light
splashing the crowd's desire. His hand
moves to the open stretch of the body's chest,
pulls it toward: "Kiss me here.
Kiss me here and here and here
and—Don't stop. Don't ever."

How Rushed They Were

The pack of boys vaulting past the porch stairs
into flight, the smell of 6 p.m.—
grass tipped with early night—seizes them
by the wrists, throat, heads dizzy.

The idea of darkness
is one they've just discovered,
small boats feeling the earth's curve,
still afloat. Suddenly, caution

is a fluorescent light over the church
basement cookie table and like cars
fearing the red light, they accelerate
into wind, grit, heave themselves

from windows, practice pitching, the taste
of insults, their dance with the safety rail.
Leaning far out into it, taking aim, they smash bottle
after bottle against the red-faced signs.

Small Boys Believing

A sink peppered in black makes a man.
A closet full of dresses is a distant country.
The night is their secret.
Backwards is an undoing.
Undoing is bad and bad is the boy
a target slapped to his back
since a middle school bathroom—
the boy they poke elbow slap push punch stomp roll high-five
over the quivering fetal lump that is not a man
simply the wallet that buys them beers
at the White Horse until they leave
cocked and needing cash.

Hiss

When I was a boy I was
the sound of a door locking—
dog left at the stairs' top,
Game Boy blinking
into the night of my room.
Waves of tiny lives
fell beneath my thumbs.
I was the hiss of static
that filled the green glow
of childhood, sliding the bolt,
turning on, waiting for the screen
that reads: *Game Starts*.

Summer in the City

Street corner, subway, stairwell—we are all
speckled with grit, slick and shining.

If there is life after death, it is this—
salt to be licked from every body.

In a storm, doors keep no secrets
and the closet empties, hangers

like question marks across the floor.
To some, the road ends at Oz;

here, we practice the art of walking
in plain sight. Let the road twist

some other's wrists. It's time
to release the stars

from their scarlet sky.
Three times. There's no place.

In the Glory Hole

A bar basement bathroom stall wall, what is
carved away, this absence you enter
hips hitting the words:

> *Put cock here*
> and
> *It just aint big nuf 4 my glory.*

It's like your penis left
for the moon, is returning
telegrams ordering gasp, clench.
Your skin prickles with shock
and then you climb the stairs
into the neon-soaked bar,
claim that well-behaved boy
hanging from a number
in the coat room,
fastening tightly at the neck.

Because

Because biology homework was too boring
and the popcorn had all been eaten.

Because the hours lay like stagnant puddles;
the rubber ducks sunken on their sides.

Because the eye exists to watch and I
owned the rights to the technology.

Because we did not share the same air
in our room.

Because skin, stroke, hand on chest,
a name.

Because lips touching is a cataclysm and fun
is a goldfish in a plastic bag.

Because she laughed when I asked, "What if?"
and touched my arm.

Because the emoticons filled the small
screen of my living.

Because I held *when* and *where* in my palm
and rolled them across the table.

Because pixels are related to pixies,
Disney, the $13 ticket.

Because discretion is a darkness;
  in the dark, I could hear them.

Because public broadcasting is as American
  as our annual turkey slaughter.

Because I was laughing
  when I pressed the button;

 my head turned to her,
  when I turned the camera on.

Viral

Did u see it? Did u? See it? See? See? See? See it? When?
Now? See it! Saw it. Did u? See u? U see u? Did. Did it.
DID. IT. Did u- yes- u- yes! Saw it. Sent it. Tweet. Tweet.
Tweet. It. He. Who? Him. Did he? Does he? He did. He is.
It. Saw it. Did he ever. LOL. How did saw it? He see it saw
it where he it saw him do it. OMG. Die. Die. Die. Would die.
How did? Would die. Why? What if? Me too! Die if. He see
him do it would die if did. Locked door. Door locked. Door
locked. Door. Locked. But. Door locked. He say see it. Again
do. Dare to. Dare you. Eye on. Eye on dresser turned on.
Turned on. Dare u. Turn on. Eyes turn on. Dareya. See. Dare
u see him now, now, right now. Didu? Go see. Him see. Didya,
didya, didya? I saw he eye on door locked do set sim das itd hit
swa sim taw swi socked sim dit ya ya ya ? Didya didya did ya
yayayayaahahahahaaaaaaaaaaaaaaaaaaaaaaaaaaaaaaaa——?

Music

When I look at sheets of music, I see a field of snow.

The notes are black dots and stems, the lines like tracks.

Still, I see snow falling—

hushed audience in the cloaked field.

Picking up the violin, I am the gross subtracted from the scene.

Even the trees are buried without their names.

ssing

he webcam showed only two men kissing.

In the eyes now
a wilderness—
when the birds open
their beaks
not in song,
but a huff
escapes from the rigor
of killing, feeding,
climbing to find,
again, the swaying
of grass, the nudging
a being makes as it moves,
no matter how
quietly, through
the world,
setting its neighbors
in motion.
How do you sleep
when the siren
is your own exhaled cry:
"Oh Christ."

Just

a lamp on
just a little lamp
a little weak lamp the kind
you put on a little table and read
really kinda dark
really dark
and we were in it
in the dark away
from the lamp in the dark
we'd been in the dark like how much
light cause we were
facing the dark like the dark
and it was a little lamp
only and it was pretty fuckin dark
and he was I thought
we it was fuckin dark right it was fuckin dark

Suite #4

There's a point
at which you can't
stand anymore. You turn
the Bach off. The cello
snouting around in your chest,
you grab by the strings and pull.
You realize the faucet has
a knob, the hallway
an exit. You take ID,
money for the train.
You turn the lights off.

Stopped I

Leave your keys in the dorm.
Leave the phone on the walk,
your wallet beside it so they will know.

Leave the note typed in the ether,
the officers in their car undisturbed,
the sound of momentum stopped.

Leave the right turn to your father,
the left to your mother,
the subway's change to your brothers before you.

Leave the music locked in its case under your bed,
the miles eaten like glass,
the chatter like flies breeding in a jar.

Leave the sight of the walkway's start—
higher now, the earth below—the rolled, kissed, handled,
shoveled, eaten, sifted, dug, packed, heavy, wishful earth—
Leave it for steel.
Leave it for air.

Leave the intersection, the bus station, the church door,
    and the exhaust.
With your back turned, there is no one there.
Leave now. It is time to walk.

Passage

People are dying all around—
leaves at October's end.
In transit, generic, something
to be raked, mulched;
they are just another job
requiring a Sunday afternoon.

Whole villages plowed under.
The work of identifying femur,
clavicle, mandible—the way children
pick shells from the sand,
demand to know their names.
It takes time, money, intention.

What's one boy's solitary fall into water
as dark as the idea of nothing?
How much splash could there be
with a boy so small losing his foothold—
not slipping, but stepping,
one foot, then a hand from the girder,
then another, out.

Phone Call

She welcomes the darkness flooding
her vision, wants only to consume
with every breath—this swimming backward.
She will simply not believe
she cannot find him, her boy
who howled when the door closed,
panicked when the nightlight burnt out.

Her hands have resurrected many things:
bottles, crayons, hats, homework, car keys,
resin, concert tickets, a forgotten password,
a silver cross. She will comb her fingers
through every tangle of weed, sift
the mountains of silt, make a net
of her body—she will simply refuse.

Waiting

Day 1

His hand covers hers
like a body thrown
over another's
to stop a blast
from shattering it
like the last time
they made love
like at any moment
she will roll,
say it was just
a car backfiring
and laugh, rising,
to hold out her hand
and pull him up.

Day 3

The kitchen light is turned on
song from somewhere like a blizzard
striking the windshield
a book of matches in hand.
What—
Where are you—
The blue water of a backyard pool
cloud singing from his mouth
how the memory
in pieces
and sleep the washing
out   spill   tide   and
crawling until nothing
beneath but air.

Day 5

This is how you make toast. Lift arms from the lap. Grip seat of chair with both hands and push body from what has held it the last three hours before dawn. Walk six steps across black tile to fridge. Lift left hand from side. Pull on freezer door and breathe deeply the cool air. Again. Breathe. Again. Look at packages of frozen food. Locate bread. Shut door. Press forehead against steel. Rock side to side. Do not think of mortuaries. Do not think of water ballooning lungs. Do not think. Realize bread is on the floor. Bend, knees popping, and wrap fingers around the plastic ruffle. Focus on gripping, tightening, gathering. Reach other hand up, grip freezer handle and pull the body upright, knees, again, popping, trailing the bread like an anchor loose from its mooring. Raise eyes and scan counters. Locate toaster in corner. Realize toaster is correct and walk. Put bread next to toaster, place both palms on cool stone and wait. Think of what is needed. Shift hips. Open drawer and slip out long carving knife. Cut through plastic wrapper, plastic inner bag, the pre-cut slices themselves. Cut the whole in half. Separate two slices. Slide them into the front two of six slots in the chrome toaster. Press black lever down until locked. Then wait. Wait. Wait for filaments to glow red. Wait. Wait. Wait for heat. Wait. Take rest of bag in hand. Stare. Turn. Walk and throw away. Put knife in sink. Return to toaster. Wait. Reach hand. Open cupboard. Slide plate from stack, lower and place beside toaster. Wait. Open drawer and remove butter knife. Remember the strawberry jam. The jam he will want when he next visits. Remember. Remember why you are waiting. Remember what you are waiting for. Stare at toaster. Breathe.

Day 7

A hospital waiting room.
My mother, yours, or—

The air is static, sludge.
Mouth squinched.
Eyes—

There is a certain kind
of pleading we associate
with animals in traps.

Belief

That your boy will be happy.
That your boy will leave your house
with a hundred packed bags
in each a marble's eye you scavenged
from a tin in the attic.
That there will be Sundays.
That your boy will be caught
when falling. That he will
exchange homes and states
and come home stating
he missed you and then hand you
his laundry and his laughter.
That he will keep his side of the bargain.

Inhale

There is a pause—
such work
to refill what
has been emptied,
the cheap squeeze
box of the
lungs insistent.
She aches from
the hundreds
of buckets. Somewhere
in the water
her son's last thought
before need
forced him
to inhale
as it soon
will force her
to do.

Tunnel

"Did you tell them that we did it on purpose?" texted
Dharun Ravi to Molly Wei.

After the vomiting,
locked door, speed dialing,
furious parents en route.
After the drugged sleep
then heaving, pleas snared
in the tunnel of her throat.
After leaning her forehead
against the cool bath
imagining another future:
high fives and back slapping,
the linger of laughter in the halls
as they all walked into a hundred nights
of futures—each different from this.
She has swallowed a black lake
in her sleep. After is now its rising.

The Secret History of Bridges

From the hurdle of Broadway
into the pinball shoot and speed
that is release—one last, long
stretch, the cyclists think,
loosening beneath the idea
of water's fingers, fresh clothes,
a drink. They are already leaving
so when they see ahead
a boy climbing the rails, it is
a fiction until
he is gone—so fast—
there—then, like all stories,
gone.

Gawker.com

*"Take the fuckin thing down," posted to Gawker regarding
an alleged photo of Tyler Clementi.*

Shirtless, faceless, arms disappearing:

there are Greek statues like this,
extremities shattered

by circumstance.
They are beautiful

as is the moth without wings
or flight:

your belly is soft,
rounded like a child's.

Everything marble-smooth.

To the Men

As he lifts, this last time,
rests the box
in the neck's curve
he recognizes the place
as where his son settled
the violin, his voice wordless
and swollen, a pressing
in the belly of hunger. Beneath
the weight of this, the father nearly
stumbles as they start
the slow march from the church
to the open mouth
of the hearse. He presses
his ear hard against the cold
slick varnish, dragging
against their progress, listening,
pressing, pressing
into this new work of waiting.

After a Long Silence

touch withdraws,
the newspaper is not passed, nor coffee, nor—
She takes the far route round the table.
When he enters, she startles as a bird will,
fleeing the thunder of his presence.
He knows he should stop this,
his job to find the door
to a language they can share
but every time he lifts an arm toward her
he stops, stares—*where
did this dead limb come from*—
and walks away.

The River

After your fragile self exploded
into a hundred drops fleeing upward.

After the river took back, closed
its mouth and swallowed.

After the men skimmed
you from a tangle of branch

and crevice. After identification
by cavity, the call, the claiming.

After students threw roses
on the very water, posted their film clips,

the blogs, comments, viewings,
linkage. After the news shifted—

the river says—*thirst*—the river says—*here*—
the river says—*sleep*.

Now What

How bodies heat each other,
the engines pressed close,
one knowing the other by its tide.

Now what, against this?
I will start at the top,
strip every picture from its nail,
graduation to birth,
until the stairs are empty.

I will hold him
in the cradle of my arms
then burn these liars
smiling from the walls.

Things You Practice

Not buying a certain brand of ham.
Not using the second check-out in the express lanes
late afternoons when the boy
with the brown eyeglass frames is packing bags.
Not answering the phone or questions.
Not buying milk.
Not pausing at the door.
Not sharing that you'd found his ghost
in a discarded shirt crumpled at the closet's back
that you'd held him to your face
that you could breathe, at last, and did
in small, careful sips, conserving.
Not sharing but waiting
for everyone to leave so you can hunt for more.

The Courts Are Shuffling Their Laws

If you subtract intention from outcome,
if you say I was not holding the oars,
if you cut the kites loose, let the dogs free,
if you drunkenly shoot in the dark

and a deer's thigh explodes
or a car is clipped
or the thrumming that is the sweet
of a summer night is silenced
and you have done this,
if you can't count that, then what?

It Is Hard to Hate the World

but possible. When sleep first recedes
and you have not yet remembered God
opened his hands and let a boy
drop—despite the Sunday donations,
the commandments kept, prayers tattooed
against the teeth—when it is still
that half-death that is half-sleep
and he is crying for Lucky Charms
and your feet are already in slippers,
body rising to answer, then,
it is possible. Then, you are awake.

Bringing Him Back

Tonight she watches her husband undress,
notices his soft belly, how he leans
to pick up his shoes, bare shoulders rounded
in the task, his glance of pride
at remembering to put things right
that he makes sure she catches.
She notes the way he walks to her
certain of a place he can rest,
seeing all she'd once hoped
for her son. She runs her fingers
through the dim ray of light
from the hall. Her husband scooping
the hand from the air as if netting a sparrow,
he presses its wild heart to his ear.

Momentum

Pills demand that you
eat your grief, stuff it into the belly
and like a final big meal
stumble from the table
eyes already dropping
conversation occurring in another room
on which the door is closing.
Slowly. Slowly.

Then, there is violence—
gun, noose, knife—a way
to punish the vehicle
that brought you here,
leave it, deserted, on fire,
roaring against the night.

But someone jumping from a bridge,
for the lasting of it, still
in movement, blind
to the destination but
moving, moving.

Less an ending
than a departure
wind stripping you to bone
so you can arrive
without a name or face.

The Persistence of Desire

The cat insists on my lap.
In her head one word:
warmth or, maybe, *safety*.
Why else does she prefer me
to the folded and deeply soft
comforter at the bed's bottom.
I am all bones, impatient. I squirm.
Yet, she is unforgiving in her focus
digging in her claws. Isn't that
what all desire is?
Cat-brained and unremitting?
I want her away. She wants
my hand on her head
and circles, circles looking for it.

Stopped II

*On viewing a Roman copy of the Greek statue "Menelaus
Supporting the Body of Patrocles" in Piazza Della Signoria
in Florence*

One man
felled,
                                    falling.

One man
holding him
    from the ground,
                        from finishing

what is always

                finished alone,

what is always
alone

                                yet

chisel in hand

he stops at the start

        of grief

where there   is
something
            still possible

to take
from the stone:

one beautiful man
                        stopped
in the arms
of another.

The Sparrow Lifts the Spent Condom into the Air

The police have been stopping
these gay, park-dark trysts

but beneath the branches,
off the path, the mulch is sharp-

scented. Strange passions
that let us flee into the rush

after the patrol car passes.
Imagine the nest built

of all our spent selves,
thin sheaths glistening

in daylight, grimed and lifted
into something else.

I Want to Give This a Happy Ending

Wings, gills, an apartment
in the Village with three guys
sharing toothpaste, stories
of a white towel dropped
at the Baths, a soundtrack
of ice chiming in a glass,
tongue outlining a set
of perfect abdominals
shuddering like a shy cat,
tracing their ridges, one man arced
over another like a wave
like fingers pushing hair
back from a forehead
like a name, a number, a door
closing on laughter
from the roommates
because before them is a new night,
another bar, party, the invitation
sitting on the kitchen table
between their outstretched arms.

Somewhere, Someone

lifts the blue help phone
from its silent cradle,
the old-fashioned heft of it
like a handle on a heavy sliding door,
how a person must insist
on it opening, feel
its movement rumble from palm
to shoulder as if the day itself
is shifting, cracking open
a space to enter, settle in, rest.
Somewhere, someone lifts the phone
and I can sleep, thinking this,
another night.

Nightmare Taken from the Closet

On viewing Petah Coyne's "Untitled #720 (Eguchi's Ghost)"
at MASS MOCA

What makes someone take an Airstream trailer,
strip it of all that is soft like peeling
the flesh from the oyster's wall, smash
then shred it until miles of silver threads unspool,
sharp as a garroting and thin as translucence?

What makes someone weave this thread—
a massive cloak, wig, shirt empty in wind,
a cave of razors, wings devoid
of embrace, the ghost waiting behind
our backs—into seize and silhouette?

Someone else has spun their veins to shine.
Someone else is gripped on hangers.
Someone else is swinging from their nightmare.
Someone else, we repeat, reading from the wall, *someone else.*

The Physics of Safety

All day, I watch the birds swoop into the green
through a tightly thatched barricade.

They arc, disappear, without harm,
everything a stillness.

I envy their precise flight. It's not
the hunger for departure

as when the city was all I dreamed,
stoned on shimmer and neon,

but their piloting between the branches,
one wing tucked close to the thrumming

inside the chest, the other tipping,
just enough. It's the need to pass

through the impassable and land
in a space I fill, exactly.

The Body's Betrayal

One morning she wakes
and a bird is pecking
at the dark wall
of her stomach, rising
into the empty space
and she begins to cry
pressing her face into the bed
for she realizes
she is hungry.

An Essential Language

i.

I remember the past:
I could not kiss
her tumbled hair,
touch her hand.
Every street corner
a foreign land.
In my desire,
I stood, gazing—
an unblinking light.

ii.

When finally there is
permission. Here,
in front of Henrietta's on 8th,
just this—my mouth
on the lips she opens
to say my name.
The city splits,
surges around us,
not even
for a moment stopping.

AUTHOR'S NOTE

Each morning, I drive over the George Washington Bridge to go to work in New Jersey. This is the bridge a Rutgers University student jumped from after his roommate broadcasted, via webcam, his encounter with another man. Although research shaped the poems, I did not know Tyler Clementi nor anyone involved in the tragedy, and I did not have access to any information other than that which was revealed through news coverage. These poems are a response to his and other similar tragedies and should not be read as fact.

RECENT TITLES FROM ALICE JAMES BOOKS

We Come Elemental, Tamiko Beyer
Obscenely Yours, Angelo Nikolopoulos
Mezzanines, Matthew Olzmann
Lit from Inside: 40 Years of Poetry from Alice James Books,
    Edited by Anne Marie Macari and Carey Salerno
Black Crow Dress, Roxane Beth Johnson
Dark Elderberry Branch: Poems of Marina Tsvetaeva,
    A Reading by Ilya Kaminsky and Jean Valentine
Tantivy, Donald Revell
Murder Ballad, Jane Springer
Sudden Dog, Matthew Pennock
Western Practice, Stephen Motika
me and Nina, Monica A. Hand
Hagar Before the Occupation | Hagar After the Occupation,
    Amal al-Jubouri
Pier, Janine Oshiro
Heart First into the Forest, Stacy Gnall
This Strange Land, Shara McCallum
lie down too, Lesle Lewis
Panic, Laura McCullough
Milk Dress, Nicole Cooley
Parable of Hide and Seek, Chad Sweeney
Shahid Reads His Own Palm, Reginald Dwayne Betts
How to Catch a Falling Knife, Daniel Johnson
Phantom Noise, Brian Turner
Father Dirt, Mihaela Moscaliuc
Pageant, Joanna Fuhrman
The Bitter Withy, Donald Revell
Winter Tenor, Kevin Goodan
Slamming Open the Door, Kathleen Sheeder Bonanno

ALICE JAMES BOOKS has been publishing poetry since 1973 and remains one of the few presses in the country that is run collectively. The cooperative selects manuscripts for publication primarily through regional and national annual competitions. Authors who win a Kinereth Gensler Award become active members of the cooperative board and participate in the editorial decisions of the press. The press, which historically has placed an emphasis on publishing women poets, was named for Alice James, sister of William and Henry, whose fine journal and gift for writing went unrecognized during her lifetime.

DESIGNED BY MIKE BURTON

⋅❧⋅

PRINTED BY THOMSON-SHORE

ON 30% POSTCONSUMER RECYCLED PAPER

PROCESSED CHLORINE-FREE

⋅❧⋅